ONE MORE BEFORE GOODBYE

Written by r.h. Sin

I like the feeling of experiencing a moment without the urge to share it with anyone outside of who was there to be a part of it. I enjoy those moments where I pick up a camera to capture something that no one else will get to see. I love the freedom of living life without anyone else to compare it to; I embrace the idea of not being liked or commented on. Sometimes it feels good not to think about a caption; I could leave it blank or post nothing at all. I like the freedom that is found in disconnecting from those small devices just to make more time to reconnect with the people I love in real life because real life is what surrounds us. Real-life can only be found when we stop looking down at phones and begin to look up at the eyes of the person who has been longing for our full attention. And so I've been practicing that right to be free as I write to be free. I am ignoring the distractions, making sure that I'm not ignoring those who deserve an interaction. Fuck being online and getting triggered when you can spend the majority of your days laughing instead of acting like everything is fine in a world that thrives off of chaos because even as the world goes to hell, there's a moment of heavenly bliss as I roll around on the carpet with my child. Being a husband made me more of who I am, and being a father has helped to secure my stance. And there is something beautiful to be found in this world when you stop allowing yourself to get lost in a sea of comments beneath a photo of someone who is just pretending to be something they're not. There is freedom in understanding that not every moment in your life is made to be consumed or critiqued or looked upon by watching eyes just for the sake of being seen. These words in this book will serve as an offering to those of you who have been so kind to me, and my only desire here is to remind you to be a bit kinder to yourself. These words are my offering to you who has often found themselves endlessly scrolling through a phone for a way out of the madness and to those who may miss my absence from their feed. I am writing this to encourage you to set yourself free because I, for one, believe that there is something that is currently keeping you from being all that you can be. And so here we are, once more just as the last time, together again as we inch closer to the last time.

I dreamed you up the other night. I saw you stronger than you've been. There was this fierce look of survival in your eyes. There was a display of strength in the way you stood there, hell at your back as the fire couldn't keep you from moving forward. It was almost as if your spirit was kindred to the flames. It would seem as though you decided to evolve despite the things that were trying to hold you back. You fought long and hard for that moment of realization, that moment where you'd finally understood what your heart was trying to tell you. Keep walking toward your light; keep running toward yourself. Your inner voice whispered. And so you pressed on, full of courage, filled with fight. Closer to triumph. I dreamed you up the other night; I saw you as the warrior you've always been. You are a conqueror of all the things that could destroy you.

No one is perfect but when you are dating someone, pay attention to how often they disregard your peace of mind and emotional well-being. Some mistakes are simply missteps, while usually, that mistake is a choice that would have otherwise remained a secret. Pay close attention to how people respond when hurting you. Many people on this earth fail to apologize or acknowledge the wrong they do but expect forgiveness and acceptance and will almost always expect you to say sorry even when you've not done a thing to them. Being human is not an excuse for being a bad person, nor should it be used in place of an apology and the act of trying to correct behavior. The people who continue to push your buttons until they get a reaction from you are not the people you should be entertaining. The people who want to determine or control how you react to their obvious bull shit are not the people you should be entertaining. Anyone who disrupts what little peace you have in the day is not a person you should be entertaining, and anyone who supports any action that distracts from being happy is not a person to be with. 99% of the relationships you experience will just be stepping stones on your way to evolving a greater sense of self-love that will require a partner to match that love and devotion or get left behind. There will be people who call themselves checking you while never really checking themselves, and those people will eventually find themselves alone with their bull shit. It is essential to identify these people as early on as you can and steer clear of them because they can and will ultimately fuck up your life.

A girl is reading this right now who still longs to be loved after years of being hurt. And so, I want to say this to you. May your scars be reminders of your survival, and may your tomorrows be stepping stones to everything you have always deserved.

I'll be honest with you. I know what your heart has felt like, I understand the disappointment that resides in your soul, and maybe I'd just like that opportunity to give you something different. You deserve something genuine, and I want the chance to part of the reason why you smile.

Walk toward the exit if you ever feel your heart is being broken by the person you love and if you can't walk, run.

I think you still have something to offer, despite the feeling of giving all that you have to the wrong person. It's not over for you, and you must not give up on finding a love that matches the one you've given to yourself.

Sometimes the wrong way is the beginning of a set of events that will help you reroute in the right direction.

she burned that bridge
just to see if you were willing
to swim toward her

I stopped wishing on the stars
the moment I gained the courage
to bet it all on the moon

You see, the night sky is a grave for stars
that have not found a way to burn as bright
as you have for as long as you have.

We build dreams in people who cause nightmares. We search for heaven in hearts that fill us up with the anguish of hell.

It's like I traded in my innocence for things I wasn't ready to feel for people who always turned out to feel nothing for me.

The nostalgia of you keeps lying to me. What I remember and what actually happened. Two entirely different stories, and I keep choosing the wrong book.

Somehow I was never enough and still too much. I kept folding myself, disappearing further and further. Made small just so that you could feel whole.

nightmares are good at pretending
to be the thing you always dreamed of

I could have been all that you would ever need, but you can't be the ocean for people who prefer mud.

I almost thought I was a ladder, the way people climb me to get to where they wanted. Left behind and stored away until they could use me again.

The lie felt good. Being told a half-truth can fill an empty cup but never enough. Those temporary highs just made coming down brutal. But empty promises always sound good to a person who is empty enough to believe them.

I have always felt lovesick for a stranger I haven't met. Endlessly searching for someone who could manage to love me in some of the same ways I've loved the wrong people.

I think it ended because we suffered long enough under this impression that staying together would somehow fix the spaces we destroyed with every argument and fight we had.

There's a crisis growing within you—a sense of doubt and disappointment. You know that leaving is best, but you decide to stay out of fear of missing out on the changes they'll make or the growth they'll experience with time. But the truth is, neither one of you will ever be able to trust one another enough to see this through. There will always be this massive sense of tension in the air. There will always be this secret of resentment growing between you both, and the only way to rediscover your smile is to leave behind the person who destroyed it in the first place.

I think I was just holding out for more time, more moments to fall in love with you, more opportunities to create memories to be relived in my dreams. I thought that if we had more time, we'd be able to fix and find everything we lost, but I was wrong. More time, more chances just meant more opportunities for you to disappoint me.

I think letting go of the wrong person is also a reward for the heart for surviving heartbreak.

We were always dancing on thin ice,
watching and waiting to see which one of us
would fall through. And without warning,
we both did at the same time, and we haven't
been able to find each other since.

What is your heart telling you right now as you read these words? And how often have you found yourself at the feet of poetry in search of solace and meaning to all the pain that lives within your soul? Where do your daydreams go to escape the hell you've experienced, and what more can I say or do to help you get away from those troubles, those rumblings, and aches inside your bones? I have tried countless times to reach you, and even though you don't always answer, I know you're reading this right now in a quiet place near the moon as the night sky becomes my stage as I calmly yell out to you. I can't help but wonder how you wander into darkness, struggling to see in front of you until you realize that you have always been capable of providing your light. You mystify me every time with your beautiful will to overcome and survive. Sometimes I like to think of myself as your guide, but at this moment, you're leading me.

Some of us leave, not to be malicious but because we realize that love can't be formed in a relationship where lies can be found in dark spaces, hidden away in hopes of never being discovered. And so I left you to find a truth that you were never really willing to tell.

I wish we could move out of this city, I'm tired of living with your ghost.

The storm was over, but it never stopped
raining in my heart.

I grew out of enjoying gifts once I realized that people buy you shit to make up for treating you like shit. I'm not too fond of this idea of people needing a reason to be kinder, especially when they often choose to put on displays of hell, setting fire to people who genuinely love them. It's almost as if the holidays become a disguise for people who spend the majority of the year hurting you. Wouldn't it be something if gifts weren't based on material items you don't actually need? Wouldn't it be nice to receive long-lasting moments where you are reminded that the person you love supports your desire for peace of mind and a life filled with love and devotion?

two people changing all at once
reconfiguring their navigational systems
to point in opposite directions

moving further from a shared dream
in an attempt to escape the nightmare
the realization that they are, in fact
in love with a person, they hate to be with

two people who have figured out
that to create peace
they must breakaway
from one another
as soon as possible

goodbyes can be sweet
leaving can be beautiful
there's hope in walking away
there's a longing in the legs
of the person who leaves
steady in pace
journeying toward
something better
in search of more
a love that doesn't require
the heart to bleed

goodbyes can be sweet
the way they push you closer
to everything you've been dreaming of
the way they move you out the arms
of the person who has become a nightmare

There was a sweet song in your absence, a melody I had not heard before I lost you. A sonic sound of freedom echoed against the walls of an empty room, once occupied by us. Losing you was the first step to finding something better to believe in.

So, thank you for leaving me the way you did. Thank you for believing that I could never do better, thank you for thinking yourself irreplaceable because it was your ego that helped me to find a peace of mind. It was your bloated sense of self that set me free and set me up to better my situation. And though you believed that you were hurting me, I healed in the moments where you no longer existed.

I believe that what is meant to remain in your life will stay and flourish and breathe joy and peace into your heart. What leaves always makes room for something more. I've been in relationships that didn't work and even in the event that I felt a sadness, the mourning becomes a celebration of the fact that not only have I always loved being alone but I also believe that failed relationships are stepping stones, some more jagged than others but always an opportunity to step higher than before. I am but an imperfect soul, often destined for heartache, sometimes little moments of happy and sometimes I've believed that I was made to be alone. But love comes and if it stays with you and it doesn't hurt to hold it then keep it for as long as you can. This life is a short film, make it beautiful with someone who wants to make it beautifully with you.

3:33
3:33
3:33
3:33

in the morning
after midnight
restless before the sun

no amount of love
can transform shit into gold

our love made of paper
torn by lies
reduced to shreds
of empty promises
and lost potential

Fuck you for looking back toward the past when what we could have made was a beautiful future together. You stared behind you so often that you lost the most honest thing that stood in front of you.

When you stop looking to your exes for something they could never give you, the journey to something better can begin.

Every time you take them back, you bury any part of yourself, and the longer you stay, the more you lose.

how ironic it is
that you set out in search of more
and found less than I gave you

made to believe
That nothing I did was good enough
made to feel
that nothing I did
would ever be appreciated

Something I've meditated on over the last decade is a desire for peace. Peace of mind is often disrupted by the people we give our time to. Something I have learned while dating. Synchronicity is hard to cultivate when you and the person you're with are on two entirely different journeys. Especially if one person has no real intention of finding themselves or evolving, some people love to break others, and some people love to help others build.

In contrast, some people love the silence of solitude that can be shared with a partner; there are some people who prefer the chaos in the arms of a disagreement that leads to a heated argument. Despite what happens, some of us want someone who brings out the best in us. Someone who wants to spend time, kick back, laugh, and talk. The dating world has been a space for games and drama, and " love " has become a mess. It's time to take back your emotional energy and refuse to give that energy to anyone who makes you feel bad or keeps you from experiencing zen, peace of mind.

If for any reason you experience a sense of calm in the absence of the person you're with. It's time to leave them.

Healthy relationships promote peace. When you're with the right person, there's a beautiful flow of positivity and inspiration daily.

If someone's absence makes you feel like you're no longer in hell, it's time to set yourself free.

Don't let broken people break your focus on what truly matters.

Marriage doesn't fix a shit relationship, and it doesn't change a person who has always chosen to be a piece of shit.

Everyone has a past, but sometimes a person's past is a pattern. PAY ATTENTION.

someday you'll learn
not to board ships
that are meant to sink

I am losing the part of me that spends most of its days making excuses to stay with you.

silence is the song
playing in the heart
of lovers who no longer
like one another

One day I will find an exit that doesn't lead me back to you.

Life will always go on without the people who made you feel like you'd never find love without them. And it is then that you will see that their absence allowed you to set yourself free.

I wish there were a cemetery
for all the love that didn't work out
I'd bury us there

It's beautiful, really, the moment it ends. The moment you lose the person you believed would be in your life forever. There's a delightful pain that occurs in the breaking up of that relationship. Most of the time, you're unaware of the beauty because you're distracted by the fear of being without that person. Still, soon enough, you realize that to get everything you deserve, you have to go without the burden of being with someone who will never deserve you.

I watched you fall for someone who made
you fall alone, and this is why I will never
love a person I can't leave.

You're just searching for someone who is after the same peace of mind you've been struggling to maintain.

You just want someone who doesn't play games, who doesn't keep you in the dark and hide you.

You just want someone genuine, someone, who isn't out to use you.

I think you're looking for someone who will match your effort, that someone you can depend on, someone who isn't lazy in the space of love.

That someone will be lucky to have found you.

I hope you find someone who isn't concerned about their ex. I hope you find someone who is so much in love with who you are in the moment that their minds aren't urged to look back toward the past.

Despite the hell beneath your feet and the storm above your head, you kept going.

Sometimes the fire doesn't hurt. There are times where the flames help forge your strength.

What I love about children is that no matter how good adults are at disguising themselves to one another, they can never bull shit a kid.

I will always love the darkness because it shows me the moon.

I wish people loved themselves as much as they hate others.

after hours spent looking at a screen
moments filled with distraction and
interruptions
is there anything left for me
is there any room for me in that head
filled with pointless current events of the
day
and useless information
that others pretend to care about
is there any time for me
once it's been wasted
on any and everything else

What if heaven is not something to only be found in death? What if you could see angels existing in the present, alive but only in acceptance and gratitude. There are moments in time that feel heavenly. Those moments where one disconnects from things that distract a person from connecting with themselves. Moments in time where one appreciates all that they have rather than aching for what they've yet to receive. What if heaven is all around us but our ability to truly touch it has been altered by our inability to refrain from romanticizing the chaos and struggle of being alive? We waste our days because we believe in tomorrow, but what if this moment is our last without warning. And it is for that reason that I decide to be free, a refusal to be dictated by the impulses and self-destructive ways of being human. And even though others may wish to bring me hell, I decide to find heaven here.

Life is a short journey and even shorter for those who are in a rush to do things that don't matter.

I've been dragging my body
through the year
with the reaper on my shoulder
hoping I'd give up

Don't you see that they're afraid of your evolution? So much that they shoot down your belief that you deserve better than what they believe you should be satisfied with. Claiming to respect your ideas, but if your thinking is indifferent to there's, they'd instead argue you into silence or proceed not to care. If you don't walk like them or talk like them or choose like them or lose like them, then something's wrong with you? Crazy, irrational. Foolish or misguided because you refuse to be led by ignorance. The wise thought to be insane, the lost pretend to be leaders while walking in circles, exploring the wrong direction. And if you refuse to follow, if you decline that invitation to be sheep. You'll get labeled blind by fake woke minds that spend most of their time asleep.

I don't argue with underachievers.

You are brilliant in the way you use your heart in search of something real even after it's been broken.

The foundation of your heart has been cracked, weakened by people who could never help you build. People who only wished to see you crumble, and even though it seems as if it'll give way, I'd like to make a home there. Not just for me but us.

mars bids for you
as the earth struggles to hold you
the night searches for you
the moon has its eye on you
and the stars dance full of light
longing for you
the sun wakes early enough
to rise and wait for you
and I'm in love with the way
you exist, planting your feet in the dirt
walking further into your own light

There are moments throughout the day when I worry about you. I'd hope that reading my words would inspire you to walk away from those who hurt you, but I know in truth that it doesn't always work out that way. And I'm not judging you for having a heart and loving that person, but I am urging you to think about your future, remember what you deserve, and stop compromising your life for someone who isn't concerned about your happiness peace of mind. And maybe you need more time; maybe it won't come as easy as you'd wish, but these words will always be at your disposal whenever you need a reminder.

Sometimes charm is a mask worn by men who only intend to use those who believe in their lies.

You're further away from the love you want, and that is because you've fallen for someone who makes you feel like you're too hard to love.

Too often, you find yourself trapped in a version of hell because you look for the good in devils who only wish to hurt you.

You look into mirrors, but you no longer recognize yourself because heartache changed you in ways you could never imagine.

You are only asking for too much when you're asking the wrong person. You are only nagging when your cries for change are shared to the ears of someone who never intended to listen to you. Pay attention to the way people respond to you. It's what they say that reveals their true intentions. The person who loves you will listen, consider, and try.

I found lies one December; I discovered betrayal that December. I remember the realization that I had allowed myself to be fooled by a weak smile and eyes that always wandered. That December was a winter hell that diminished my belief in love. I vowed that December never to kiss the lips of a liar. I promised myself to avoid the entertaining of anyone who would bring my heart destruction and chaos. I declared an unwillingness to build my hopes and dreams on nightmares. Winter arrived once more, the following year, and this was when you appeared. Somehow in my darkest hour, you walked in like a torch, a freedom flame. A light that I could follow in the night, more beautiful than the moon. A stranger full of delight, full of promise, you came to save me from the lies. And I will always love you endlessly.

I love life because you love me; thank you,
Samantha.

in front of heaven, outside of hell
somewhere steady in between
my feet are off the ground
the air engulfs my lungs
my arms stretched in both directions
my eyes fixated forward
my mind gives in to yesterday

where am i
who am i
where do i go
where is home

1271125